Things You Think I Don't Know

Deborah Kay Davies has been writing and publishing poems and short stories for the past ten years. *Things You Think I Don't Know* is her first full-length collection of poetry.

Things You Think
I Don't Know

Deborah Kay Davies

Parthian
The Old Surgery
Napier Street
Cardigan
SA43 1ED

www.parthianbooks.co.uk

First published in 2006
© Deborah Kay Davies 2006
All Rights Reserved

ISBN 1-905762-21-6
        978-1905762-21-7

Cover design by Marc Jennings
Inner design by www.lloydrobson.com
Printed and bound by Dinefwr Press, Llandybïe, Wales

Published with the financial support of the Welsh
Books Council

British Library Cataloguing in Publication Data
A cataloguing record for this book is available from the
British Library

Contents

Heron

I had this long dream
smelling of frog-spawn.
It was full of feathers
that brushed my bare shoulders
like rainy ferns,
and thin, funnily-hinged legs;
I had a feeling of being trampled.
There was a snaky shape
weaving about.
I kept seeing shining, flat eyes.

Eventually, I made it to morning,
stretched my arms, yawned,
and saw a heron
sitting in the wide-open bedroom window.
Its compact head
pushed the curtain to one side;
its neck described a question mark.
Webbed feet, the colour of old egg yolks,
hung down in rubbery folds
against the radiator.
Giving me one serious look,
then pivoting its head outwards,
it launched off inelegantly.
Breast feathers like flakes of new sky
floated onto the carpet.
A breeze blew in from the river
and lifted my fringe.

Then I noticed:
on the other side of the bed,
in a nest of ripped pillows,

sat a huge, pale-blue egg.
I put my ear to the still-warm smoothness
and heard a knocking sound,
someone calling my name.
A piece of shell fell on the duvet.
I put my eye to the chink.
Is that you? I said.

Don't Mess With Mermaids

Her arm around a flaky pier leg,
cracking limpets off to crunch,
she lolls in gulping,
blood-black tide,
turns the blind,
salt-crusted stare of a seal
on anyone who comes so near.

Her submerged hair spreads
like octopus ink,
alive with a meandering swarm
of radiant sea-snails.
In the centre of her broad forehead
a starfish sucks.

She throws her head back
and yawns,
kneading her belly
just where the scales
turn soft,
yearning for the gristle
of young sailors,
their hot, tacky juice.

Wings

I followed her upstairs
and saw piles of rubbish
spread across the floor-boards.
It's been hard
to find the time, she said.
Now I'm fixing these together
with strands
of my dear children's hair.
I've been collecting it for years.
See, his springy, blond locks
for weightlessness,
hers, straight and black,
for strength.
I've used many things
in this construction.
Two types of chain,
fine and heavy,
perfect for the harness;
old irons, shelves from the oven;
thinnest shavings of skin
from the back of the one I loved.
I did it in the night,
he never woke.
Gold rings; perfume bottles;
pieces of the mirror
I smashed seven years ago;
the arms of my father's glasses;
the tip of the tongue
my mother lied with;
the head of the doll
my sister stole, perfect for a prow-head;
silk slips, dried roses, baby teeth.

This crocheted shawl; love letters,
all used for ornament.
I've utilised certain extracts from my diaries;
grey, white, black days, a few crimson,
to provide much-needed lift.
Be my witness, she said:
whatever the wind's direction,
I fly out tonight.

Auntie's Place

Back to the billowing garden
washed in a gaudy, wall-flower delirium,
where the raspberry bursts and oozes
in a course of brightest blood
to track and mimic
warm, blue veins in a thin white wrist,
sole witness to a trespass.
Back to the sneezy geranium,
and the cat that lies drugged
in its own hot pool of black and violet fur.

The enclosing stones drone with heat.
Heavy-headed roses droop
and yearn for moisture.
Butterflies blunder and creak
through a sweet syrup of perfume,
drowsily knocking the dust
from faded hollyhock knots,
candied and scrunched now,
brittle as crepe paper.

A slow-motion, carpet-slippered wait
for small, sugared tomatoes,
nestling in leaves of damp mint,
and glistening fruit
in fluted amber dishes
with wafer-thin bread for the juice.
And angel-cakes that float
on crackling cloth-clouds
in tongue-melting swathes
of palest lemon and pink.

The walnut piano after tea
and always the clotted lilac,
deathly-sweet,
that breathes itself
on knuckles knobbed and stiff,
but able still to ease out
those boned, long-skirted tunes,
while the evening faces
in their silver frames smile down.

From the open, mothy window
the homely woods are piles of dusky pillows
wafting and tumbling one on the other.
Only I know the secret of that bare summit
where the devil built his wicked heap of stones
with seared and scaley hands.

The piano is silent;
the frames are blank.
There is no one left but me
to walk the little paths and lean to dodge
the swaying swags of dew-hung phlox.

Allotment Time

Now he burns drooping plants.
You've got to root things out, he says.
Smoke smudges the bluebell pools beyond.
A blackbird sings,
meshed in a twiggy bush.
Sharp notes score the branches.
Each note leaves
a lime-green clot.

Now he jabs the earth awake,
each spadeful juicy
as steamed ginger pudding.
Chopped worms writhe bluntly;
for them the air is acid.
In a threat of wings,
swarthy, ochre-eyed,
the blackbird swoops.

Over there,
inside stands of calm hedging,
thrushes describe the twilight
to perfection.
Wiping his brow on a spotted rag
he says, *get in quick*.
I squat in the wheelbarrow,
and smell him behind me:
creosote, string, sweat.

Hymn Singing

She's spent a lifetime
in this creaking, sticky-backed pew
between her mum and dad.
Sung the hymns.
Melodiously owned she was destined,
well before the world's
foundations were built,
to be a guilty worm,
a filthy rag,
a pig-swill guzzling sinner
masquerading in her best coat.

Cow's-lick burnished
with her mother's spit,
she's sweated and harmonised
about her position as a brand
snatched from the burning,
counted her many blessings,
saw what God has done,
shunned evil companions,
disdained bad language,
kept the yawny Sabbath Holy, Holy.

Now she's coming up to fifteen.
Lately it was agreed
she should have a trainer bra.
She's beginning to hope that soon
the gold-spun door
of that bright home
for wispy-winged children
above the clear blue sky,

will clang shut on her
once and for all.

She bites her short top lip
as she thinks about how she'll
shed her bulky undies
and plunge head-first,
whooping with joy,
into those dark, volcanic passions,
those heats of desire,
those fleshly lusts
she's been cautioned nightly about.
If only she can find them.

Instep

She was fifteen,
climbing rocks with friends.
Squirming as barnacles
pierced the balls of her feet,
she slipped down the slime
of bottle-green pools,
grazed her shin
on a stretch of molluscs,
lay on her front
and watched purple sea-things
open and close,
open and close.

Then she fell,
cut her instep deeply.
It didn't hurt or bleed,
she was so cold.
They carried her back,
settled her with cushions,
and went swimming.

Feeling light-headed,
the beach-sounds fading,
she cradled her foot
in both chilled hands
and gingerly pulled apart
the whitening wound to look,
then held her breath,
shocked at how like
a sea-creature
she was inside.

Things You Think I Don't Know

She whispered:
our mother's cunt
is like the eye of a lizard,
bleared and slow,
sunk in a goose-flesh socket.
At times it drips funny-coloured tears
that burn small holes
in the edges of our mummy's skirts.

You've observed
those lacy patterns in the hems?
Well, now you know.

She told me:
our father's prick
is as long as a dingo's
and easily as whippy.
When his hind legs fold,
it drags on the floor.

You've seen how daddy winces
when he hunkers down
to play with us?
Well, now you know.

She said:
your seed and mine,
black as two olive stones,
dropped from our father's ear
into our mother's silver throat
while she sang to him
one cat-calling night.

You've heard those
raspy sounds she makes?
We ripped her cords
when we were born.
So now you know.

Weird Hole

I was in town with Wendy.
As we came out of Marks and Spencer's
she was updating me
on the progress
of her embarrassing rash,
when I heard this screeching sound
and the pavement opened
right in front of my feet.
Naturally, I stopped and peered in.
There was a rush of damp air.
I could hear water plinking.
Some bloke shouted echoingly from far below,
come and join me, it's party-time down here.
It sounded like a pretty silent party.
As if, I yelled back,
and edged around the wobbling slabs.
I could use some cigarettes, he called,
sounding crestfallen.
I've given up, I bellowed over my shoulder,
and hurried to catch up with Wendy.
Wow, Wendy, I said,
*how unexpected, you know,
the way that hole just, like, appeared
in front of M and S.*
She turned and frowned at me.
What hole? she said.

Test

I had to go for a cytology test.
I'd put it off for months, as you do.
The Sister said, *OK, here's the drill;*
slip off your panties,
pop on the couch,
and assume the position.
Oh, and try to relax.
She was quite a comedienne.
Bending down between my legs,
she was just about to ask
if I'd booked my summer hols yet,
when instead she stood back quickly.
Hello, she breathed,
I thought I'd seen most things in my time,
but this takes the biscuit.
I sat up.
Is there anything wrong? I asked.
Well, don't freak, she said,
but I see two old people up there.
What do they look like? I said.
She bent to have another look,
and extricate her instrument.
The woman's wearing white sandals,
and those icky sockette things;
the old guy's waving a newspaper.
Did you notice which one? I asked.
She sighed and had another shifty.
The Telegraph, she said, turning away.
That's my mum and dad I said.
Any messages?
The Sister was trying to keep her voice casual.
Your mum's saying something

about a nice strong cup of tea
and a sandwich.
I can't say I blame her.
What does my dad say? I asked.
She was at the sink by now, washing her hands.
All your dad wants
she said, *is his mac.*

Insect

She's lying in an old oak bed,
but really this is about centipedes.
The room's festooned with them.
They smell like liquorice,
only more rooty.
Some have beards,
some are sterner than others.
One has the face of Dean Martin,
but they all make her shudder,
even the one thin as a French bean
who abseils from the ceiling,
a beetle gripped between his jaws
like a rose.

As centipedes drop out of the curtains
they sound like falling All-Bran.
Soon they writhe in shiny
mounds on the floor-boards.
She thinks she'll scoop them up
but nothing is to hand.
The mounds gradually quieten down.
It seems they are snoozing.
For this, at least, she's grateful.

As the room dims,
(a nest of young centipedes
has covered the only light-bulb like a hat),
she discovers a twelve-inch granddaddy
on her pillow.
She's paralysed of course,
but mentally she shrinks away.
He rears up and weaves

like a creaky, vermilion cobra
in front of her narrowed eyes,
insinuates himself around
between the pillow and her bare neck.
His touch is like Velcro.
As he snags her hair,
and deposits something gunky
underneath her jaw,
she whispers: *I will not accept*
I wear you like a scarf.
And anyway, this is just a dream.

He tightens his grip
when he arrives in front of her nose again,
then tunnels through her flesh,
just above the Eve's-apple.
He's inching up her windpipe.
Her mouth flies open.
Where her tongue was, there he is.
Come on boys,
he says in a voice like wet toadstools
to the glinting crowds of centipedes
watching breathlessly around her prone body,
help yourselves.

This Is The One

This is the one
where she runs
down a corridor
holding her children's
soft, waxy hands,
and Elvis is crooning
are you lonesome tonight,
and her long skirts
are bulky and noisy,
like that cheap sleeping-bag
she bought from a discount store.

In her ears, the sound
of rushing water.
Underfoot,
plush red carpet shrinks
from the skirting boards,
revealing two strips
of a glittering,
murderous, full-pelt river.
She peers down, down
to where long, grinny sharks flick.
They are upholstered
in the very same material
as her new lounge curtains.
But their teeth are
David-Attenborough, sharky ones.
They snap their jaws peckishly,
rolling over and over.

Both children
slip from her grip

and shoot away
beneath the water's green surface.
Their huge eyes blink slowly,
their blond hair waves goodbye.
As they disappear
they wag baby index fingers.
This is what happens, they yell,
this is what happens
to mothers who

After Birth

There's a hovering in the air.
A white-gowned acolyte,
her murmur barely rising
above the rasp of tearing lungs,
offers solemnly
a tray of shiny instruments
glistening with moisture.

Look now, this long, curved piece
is pushed up along one side,
and the other likewise.
Then we pull.
The kiss of raw, ice-tongued steel
on shrinking flesh.

(Galileo, you were right to recant
on your tour of the dungeons.
See – here, the thumb-screws,
here the red-hot pincers –
cool now, of course...)

Silently, toward evening,
she appears once more,
a plum-red votive offering,
grainy and lumpen, on a silver salver.
Eyes greedy,
reluctant to share,
look, she says, *look*.

A private cradle for a blind thing,
crouching in its own puddle,
dark-veined, secret, inner,

riddled with wispy threads of indigo,
shot through with dull cream and pewter.
Rolling and kneading it with her fists,
No, she says, *look*

January Park

The swan's legs
were trapped overnight.
All day yesterday
an effervescent wind
choreographed the snow.
Now the lake gapes
from its fringe
of black fern
like a moonstone walleye.

At midday
a small child,
chill-giddy under the rimy trees,
frou-frous in the snow,
runs bulkily over the rise.
I see him falter,
strain to look back,
trip on his red scarf,
bowl faster down.

No sound
as the lake's eye
blinks once.
Under the ice
waves a tiny crimson hand.

Alfresco

Suddenly, someone's up in the lime trees
feeding strings of seed pearls
into the wine glasses,
knocking the crust from my bread.
You dash away across the lawn
to bloom with the other umbrellas
under a spruce canopy.

Empty chairs, silent tables.
My white bowl brims with spring water.
Two young sprigs of beech
circle like strange fish.
The melting leaves dangle
citrus perfume on my head.

Alone, I watch tiny snails,
striped like antique mints,
glide up the lacquered twigs
of a potted bay tree.

The Otamak Eat Earth

And tell about the usefulness of doubting.
They call me 'traveller without a shadow'.
Take heed, they say,
all animals celebrate the full moon.
The jaguar is our shaman.
Flowers take flight:
crimson, flame and dark-wine.
The Otamak show me harmless,
black-skinned vipers
who feed on venomous snakes.
Above us the forest exhales oxygen.
The Otamak hold spears, bend low,
request forgiveness
from fish with fins like human hands.

We take only to fill our bellies, they sing.
We are all one: hungry, naked, grieving.
They hold up brother stone,
smash brittle fish skulls;
at sunset roast dense flesh
on wet cinnamon twigs.
They bring spiked palm leaves,
poisoned with curare,
show how to bind them round
elbows and wrists.
We mortally wound our enemies
in hand-to-hand combat.
We give the captured man
his sister's daughter, they say,
then he is slaughtered and eaten.

In the rainy season
I listen to the wild boar herds
grind their teeth and snore.
The Otamak explain
how to make a shelter
of palm hearts and aspidistra.
They tell me it is lucky to host many bats in them,
laughing behind their hands.
Surrounded by frogs big as boxer puppies,
I tell the Otamak stories about snow.
The Otamak speak words,
mouths flickering in the fire-light.
They tell me my way back is barred.

Gotham City

Saturday night.
Frank's Plaice
burps a breath of fat and vinegar.
Sharon's tights have run;
Darren's boil burst on the bus.

Posses of hefty, arm-linked girls,
fringes like barbed-wire,
parade the length of Market Street,
hair-spray cans
like loaded guns in their fists.

Darren's moussing his hair in the toilets,
boil winking in the half-light.
He watches, wistful,
as the boys do the town-circuit,
safe in their Ford Fiestas,
revving with gusto in the gutters,
furry cubes a-jiggle.
He hears the girls squeal on cue.

It's Saturday night
and Darren's hoarded dole needs spending.
Who knows? He might just pull tonight.
His palms are swampy,
but he's trying to lounge
on the door-jamb of The Labour In Vain,
eyes narrowed, lips shaped to a silent whistle;
you have to wait on Saturday nights.
'Round the corner
Sharon's pumping her hair-spray can.

Overboard

Lots of families on this boat.
The voyage will be long;
easily a lifetime.
At least, that's what the brochure said.
Mothers hang hand-washed, fraying nappies
from every available rope.
It's hard to take a stroll
without being thwacked in the face
by a faintly urinous rag.
Everyone is making do.

The children keep busy
as only children can:
hopscotch, picking each other's scabs,
beating up the smaller ones,
comparing body parts,
snogging, nicking. The usual.
My own kids I never see.
This is a seriously big boat.

The men meet in black groups.
They form committees.
Someone gets murdered.
I'm not sure if that's true –
rumours multiply like germs –
but I did hear a loud splash once in the early hours,
body-heavy, if you know what I mean.

My husband tells me every night
about minutes and proposals,
people seconding motions.
As he cleans his teeth

he says *there needs to be a new regime*.
He bares his foaming teeth in the mirror, sucks in,
says *what this boat needs*
is a strong man in charge.

I've come to like weevils.
They supply texture
and much-needed roughage.
Provisions, though;
apparently, we've got enough for eternity.
I'm already sick of fish.
To be honest,
I'd kill for a sausage.

It's the January of our third year
and I've started leaning out to sea.
I don't do anything, just lean.
And search for anything spiky.
Anything not rolling and greenly heaving.
I long for a multi-story car-park,
perhaps a telegraph pole.
I know it's not going to happen.

Then, one day, I look down instead.
No reason, perhaps I'd given myself
a crick in the neck with all that gazing.
I see something floating up to me
from deep below.
It stops just inches from the surface.
I must be going nuts, I think.

There, grinning, is a little merman.
He's fluttering his hands about.
Presumably to stay in one place.
I notice he has very flexible wrists
for a fifty-something.
His tail is fabulous.
He's had it decorated with sea-anemones.
They flutter their hands too.

He has a belly like Van Morrison.
I suppose there's no reason
why a merman shouldn't,
but it throws me a bit.
Also, a long, frondy beard
and reddish moustache.
He's bald, and there are small, shiny crabs
crawling over his pate.
It's probably a mer-fashion thing.
I hold onto the railings till my hands go numb.
This is so bizarre.

He gestures to me.
He's saying *leave the ship*.
Leave all that behind.
Come on. Jump.
I think he fancies me,
though it's hard to tell with mermen.
His eyes are the wettest, truest blue.
He looks like fun, somehow.

I climb up and straddle the top rail.
My hair is slapping my cheeks.
From the galley I hear the dinner gong,
and realise I'm starving.
The merman's arms are spread wide,
he's winking in an exaggerated manner.
Still, I feel he'll catch me.
I swing my other leg over;
the sea is sucking my toes
as I'm poised on the rail.

Second Thoughts

They're travelling up-country
on a second honeymoon.
The first was strange enough:
he, crying for his parents,
she for the green chiffon nightie
she'd fondly bought
in Marks and Spencer's,
thinking it glamorous,
thinking it seductive;
he had judged it to be
in extremely poor taste.
You should know
I'm strictly
a white lawn man, he'd said.

Now, on the train,
she thinks of tight,
orange rosebuds,
how they wilted so early.
She's remembering
borrowed perfume,
the way it clung
to her gown's bodice
and wafted with her
down the aisle.
She'd thought the aroma
beautiful, romantic.
He said it seemed
to trigger off
his asthma,
though he couldn't be sure.

Curtains

I'm sure that the moth,
blind and heavy,
covered in down
like a large pussy willow,
which incessantly
bludgeons its blunt head
at my lamp-lit window,
has the familiar face
of the one I love.
So why am I so quick
to snap shut the curtains?

Sunday Morning

While she's in the bathroom
he sits up
and hastily comes into his hankie.

She perches on his side of the bed
and strokes his arm
as she makes a phone call.

Sunbeams slice billowy curtains;
Tammy sings from the radio.
Shall I plunge? he asks.

His hand is on the coffee-pot lid.
I think it's perked, he says.
Deep in conversation, she nods.

Like a guarantee of good times
coffee aroma fills the room.
He reads the paper.

Only the top of his head is visible.
On the phone, her friend asks
how things are working out.

We're okay so far, she says,
and idly wipes her nose
on the discarded hankie.

She gives no sign
as she detects its smell of earth and ocean,
feels cold gunk on her upper lip.

Behind her blue eyes
four bars of an ancient electric fire
click full-on and hum savagely.

She puts the phone down
without saying goodbye,
and waits to see what he will do.

In one fluid movement
he takes the handkerchief from her hand,
palms it into his dressing-gown pocket,
and asks if she has any plans for the day.
No, she says.
No definite plans yet.

Hello?

Once, I choked in the street
on a slender grey bone.
Retching,
I ran to a phone box
and called you.

Hello? You said,
from your office
in another city
forty miles away.

At the time,
as I clutched the handset,
and knelt
coughing bubbles of blood,
I felt you could help.

Consuming Passion

It's not enough for me
to kiss my lover's mouth
long and hard.
I want to eat his tongue and lips.

To stroke my darling's weary head
is only half of what I want.
Better to peel back his scalp,
and with my bright pin
pick out thoughts,
packed dense,
like pomegranate seeds.

I'm not complete
when my arms strain
his dear frame close and close.
I want to watch my rib-cage open out
and smoothly draw
my love inside the steam and glow.
Our entrails entwining,
heart beside jumping heart.

Saying It With Flowers

Suburban night-shade.
She lies and smiles,
double-bedded,
straight, untrue,
intent on revelation;
the bouquets are emerging
from deep inside.
Garlands of mauve bruises
bloom around her right breast;
fat pansies, blue and cream,
appear on the cool skin
a handspan above her knee.
Posies of forget-me-nots
encircle her upper arms.
A lover's gifts,
Intra-flora.

Devotions

She bows her head,
clasps her hands and kneels,
pressed hard and strong and secret
by the heavy finger of desire.
Make no mistake,
it's not for mercy that she cries,
but more.

The Knowledge

You think I don't know
you think that now it's just the two of us again,
there's a chance our life will expand,
flare into Technicolor, Judy-Garland-dazzle us.

You talk of Harley-Davidsons, Spain, galleries, films,
the ocean, the desert, delicious food;
you say *Langoustines! Asparagus! Cheese! Cream! Wine!*
Like a loving little devil you take me up, up, up,
and wave your arms about.

You show me books, log-fires, Gene Kelly,
things you know me well enough to know I'll want.
All my love, you shout,
hanging on for dear life,
for ever and ever!

You think I don't know
how you stay awake at night
and play a secret tape next to my sleeping ear.
You think I don't know it intones,
please stay, please stay, please stay,
please…

Over

Quite free, this once, to do so,
she phones him from her home.
In the unlit hallway
she shivers uncontrollably,
her throat a soft, pink tunnel,
closing in.
On the line his voice
is a warm coat wrapping her up.

It feels like November.
They take their last walk
around a nettle-edged lake,
its waters inky,
scalloped by small winds.
Sweet-wrappers flap
in the holly branches.
Pleasure boats, half-submerged,
have pock-marked hulls,
their chains strike just the right note.

It starts to rain.
They stop to face each other, hold hands.
An empty Coke can rolls into a ditch.
She feels she carries
many people on her back,
but can not put them down.
She loves him
as he tells her
he understands;
no need for words.

Nought

These dying, seedy August days,
still rattling on about picnics and beaches,
and the punctuation of a mutual anniversary:
fluted fiery tiger-lilies
bleeding into spotted amber hearts,
scentless Audrey Hepburn rosebuds
like little orange studs
pinned on ramrod straight stems.

Through the bars of a florist's wiry foliage
I listen hard like someone emerging from a long
and weakening illness
as he tells with words as sweet as glowing nectarines
of so much stronger love.
But from where I stand
the horizon looks flat and chilly,
the prospect as empty and ominous
as a row of flashing noughts that pulse
on an abandoned, idling video machine.

She's Grateful For The Mist

Released by her crushing fingers,
sharp, limy smells of curled-up fern tips
cut through the sweet biscuit breath
of dry grass
and an oil slick of sheep smoke.

The barbed-wire shriek of a peacock
tears at a memory, faint and early.
For a moment she is plunged,
like a witch in a sack,
back into the watery night.

If it weren't for this heat-haze
you could see things
clearly from this point, he says.

Useful mist...
obscuring horizons,
limiting vision...

Her Week

Eat quarter of a bowl
of seafood pasta;
the mussels look like
tiny, excised cunts.
Note to self:
no interest now felt
about eating that type of thing.
Also, all three tomato-hued prawns
could have been
severed human ears.

Buy pair of fishnet tights;
colour: aubergine, apparently.
They rupture as pulled on.
Instep still painful from prongs of plug.
For future ref:
false nails, though dramatic,
are detrimental
to delicate fabrics.
Uncomfortably bleak truth:
medium hosiery
now proving inadequate;
sizing's a minefield.

Break down and weep
sitting in strobey, twilit cinema
listening to the soundtrack
on a Jaguar advert:
Roy-Orbison-meets-Edith-Piaf-type voice.
Interesting sum –
fast cars plus certain music
plus cinema snacks

invariably equal brief despair.
Question: could it have been
the popcorn that smelt farty?

Perform daily power-walk.
In bedraggled park,
hide behind bald tree
and greedily watch poodle
run in circles like black, athletic lamb,
a good long way
from unappreciative owner.
Pat on self's back;
super-human restraint employed
in struggle not to scoop up dog,
conceal under
voluminous woolly,
and leg it home.

Awaken at three-thirty AM.
Bedroom curtains
blocks of orange neon.
Slide out of bed,
pick up large pebble,
invaluable as door-stop.
Drop it on his exposed foot
to rouse.
Then hold said pebble
in two hands above head,
firmly announcing,
I know this sounds harsh,
but shove off
until that thing gets better.

Repeat to oneself
each night on retiring:
decide it,
sort it,
feel like a new woman.

What It's Like

It's like the evening
I locked the bathroom door,
took a deep breath,
and yanked my heart out.
Amazed at how far its pipe-work
trailed across the tiles,
way beyond the dry-sob stage,
I reeled it in
then sat with my hands full
and watched the blood-blurts slow,
the twitching stop.

Crossing the lounge
like someone leaving a car wreck,
I tried to keep hold
of the flailing, bloody tubes
with my fingers.
Kneeling down by his slippered feet,
here, I said with difficulty,
(my mouth gone square-shaped)
here's how much.

From behind the newspaper
his hand appeared
and firmly stubbed
a cigarette out
on my heart's cheek.

On Fridays I Go Down

Like a leaf
on a sure spin;
red frills,
crisp curve,
jewel glints,
copper bend.

Pretty, yes,
only still down,
still falling;
a weekly burrow
like a screw
into wood.

But soft too,
like a faulty foetus
is swaddled by
living saline blankets;
gripped
in an incontrovertible,
slick descent.

And rooting,
busy,
bored;
true as a germ
in an endless
wound.

There Is Always The River

She wakes, climbs from a wide, warm bed,
sheds her soft nightgown.
Wet things call:
serrated rub of brambles,
irresistible slap of giant knot-weeds,
flail of mature ferns stirred by wind.
Her mind is moving down
near slugs, snails, worms,
level with small pools flowering rain,
then up in the lovely, sodden trees,
running surefooted, tiptoed, along shining branches,
on the familiar route.

Soon the river,
its smell of oil and trout,
exuberant, tumbling stones,
ducks still as rocks along the margins.
She walks at one with all night-things
that long to enter water.
Rain-drops are like slate-flakes
thrown on her bare breasts,
streaming belly, steady flanks.

She pauses at the river's edge,
lies down on grass ropy
as the saturated manes of ponies,
and drapes her arms in its fringe,
smells marginal plants,
listens to the darting, stop-start
conversation of minnows.
Then she rolls down,
splices the black shine,

turns and turns, shredded by flints,
ripped by trailing creepers,
bluey-green, uncaring in the moonlight.

She is waiting, as she drifts and rolls,
for the weir,
the tumbling coke cans and bottles,
doll's-heads and writhing nests of twine,
her long, nightly dance
in its indifferent, roaring lap.

That's Nothing

Mine is like
the drained,
crack-tiled
outdoor swimming pool
of a November Butlin's;
in the deep end
leaves rustle like discarded skins.
A deflated li-lo scuttles.

Mine is like
the single child's trainer
you see briefly,
its tongue flopping
in the stiff grey grass
of the motorway's
central reservation
as you scream past.

Mine is like
an elephant's graveyard.
Think about how
those empty rib-cages
howl at the unmoved sky;
spinal cords; stiff trunks;
huge pulpy stinks;
plip plip plip as things liquefy.

Mine is like
an abandoned rugby stadium.
The howl and wail of old hymns.
Hot piss streams evaporated.
All those cans flattened.

The goal posts yawning
like portals
to an underworld.

On The Night She Saw A Frog

The pavements were shining
like the backs of seals,
and it could have been a leaf,
or a turd,
but she felt an assurance
it was not.
And they were walking fast,
not speaking,
breathing hard
through their silent mouths,
walking from something,
trying not to run,
though they wanted to;
but perhaps
in different directions.

The glowing house windows
all spoke to her of canaries
settling in their breast feathers,
cheese on toast maybe.
And she knelt down
to see the still frog,
wanted to hold it,
knowing that was wrong,
the frog being so dignified
there on the pavement.
But she was afraid it would jump –
leave her in the black and orange street –
so grabbed its cold, straining leg
that looked like the long-muscled
sheathed leg
of a male ballet dancer,

and held on,
trying not to squeeze,
just exert enough pressure
to make it stay.

The puddle she knelt in
seeped into her jeans,
and she blushed because the frog
used its other leg
to try and get away from her,
like a biker
kick-starting his engine.
She watched the frog's snub head,
its little throat working,
mouth a narrow, dark crack,
eyes like millions
of other frog's eyes,
but for the fleck of street-lamp
at each shining centre,
that eloquent, scrabbling leg,
and knew she had to let go.

Her Boat

She is with her father
in the front-room
with its pair of chipped china owls
and the photos of missionaries
wearing bouffant hair-dos
who all seem to balance
their mawkish lapfuls of offspring
with other-worldly indifference.
He's been telling her all about them
struggling against things
in Papua New Guinea;
or in some jungle with an airstrip
thin as an Elastoplast,
three-hundred miles from their mud hut.

Her mother is in the kitchen
talking, talking;
to the clock, to the oven,
to the water-logged cactus,
wherever God is this evening.
After a lengthy grace
they all eat together
at the G-Plan table.
Dessert is rice-pudding.
Her mother again expresses surprise
when she declines a bowlful.

Her father is spectacularly burdened.
Of course, he says,
sighing over his tea cup
as if it were the fallen world,
it has been a tough winter,

what with the weather,
my chest, your mother.
And then what you did.
I was deeply wounded
by what you did, you know.
Perhaps I'll never get over it.
His pills are on the side-table she bought them.

She looks out of the window
and thinks, no, I won't take this on board.
More and more she sees herself
as a small, Arthur-Ransome-type boat,
shrugging off choppy waters.
But driving home, weaving through
road-works, demisting the windows,
she senses that rat darting
up the mooring ropes, bringing his friends.
All of them gleeful, ratty,
ready to nest, increase,
weigh her boat down,
chew it up.

Acknowledgements

Many of these poems first appeared in *New Welsh Review*, *Planet* and *Poetry Wales*; acknowledgements are also due to *Reactions 2: New Poetry Anthology* (University of East Anglia) and *The Pterodactyl's Wing, Welsh World Poetry* (Parthian).

I would like to thank The Arts Council of Wales for the writer's bursary I received to complete this book.

Thanks to Tiffany Atkinson, Jane Blank, Karen Buckley, Anne Cluysenaar, Bryn Daniel, Roger Ellis, Colin Evans, Danny Gorman, David Greenslade, Hilary Llewellyn-Williams, Ruth Smith and Jim Tucker.

Special thanks to Camilla, Edmund and Howard for their invaluable support, and the garden shed I loved.

Finally, thanks to Norman.